The Thirteen Articles of Faith

A Declaration of Belief, of Members

of
The Church of Jesus Christ
of Latter-day Saints

With Observations by
Phil Hudson

Copyright 2017 by Philip M. Hudson.
The book author retains sole copyright
to his contributions to this book.

Published 2017.
Printed in the United States of America.

All rights reserved.

No portion of this book may be reproduced, stored in a retrieval system, or transmitted in any form or by any means – electronic, mechanical, photocopy, recording, scanning, or other – except for brief quotations in critical reviews or articles, without the prior written permission of the author.

ISBN 978-1-943650-51-5

Illustrations – Google Images.

This book may be ordered from
online bookstores.

Published by BookCrafters
Parker, Colorado.
www.bookcrafters.net

The Thirteen Articles of Faith

1. We believe in God, the Eternal Father, and in His Son Jesus Christ, and in the Holy Ghost.

2. We believe that men will be punished for their own sins, and not for Adam's transgression.

3. We believe that through the Atonement of Christ, all mankind may be saved,

by obedience to the laws and ordinances of the Gospel.

4. We believe that the first principles and ordinances of the Gospel are: first, Faith in the Lord Jesus Christ; second, Repentance; third, Baptism by immersion for the remission of sins; fourth, Laying on of hands for the gift of the Holy Ghost.

5. We believe that a man must be called of God, by prophecy, and by the laying on of hands by those who are in authority, to preach the Gospel and administer in the ordinances thereof.

6. We believe in the same organization that existed in the Primitive Church, namely, apostles, prophets, pastors, teachers, evangelists, and so forth.

7. We believe in the gift of tongues, prophecy, revelation, visions, healing, interpretation of tongues, and so forth.

8. We believe the Bible to be the word of God as far as it is translated correctly; we also believe the Book of Mormon to be the word of God.

9. We believe all that God has revealed, all that He does now reveal, and we believe that He will yet reveal many great and important things pertaining to the Kingdom of God.

10. We believe in the literal gathering of Israel and in the restoration of the Ten Tribes; that Zion (the New Jerusalem) will be built upon the American continent; that Christ will reign personally upon

the earth, and, that the earth will be renewed and receive its paradisiacal glory.

11. We claim the privilege of worshipping Almighty God according to the dictates of our own conscience, and allow all men the same privilege, let them worship how, where, or what they may.

12. We believe in being subject to kings, presidents, rulers, and magistrates, in obeyimg, honoring, and sustaining the law.

13. We believe in being honest, true, chaste, benevolent, virtuous, and in doing good to all men; indeed, we

may say that we follow the admonition of Paul – We believe all thing, we hope all things, we have endured many things, and hope to be able to endure all things. If there is anything virtuous, lovely, or of good report or praiseworthy, we seek after these things.

The Road to Riches

Faith

Repentance

Baptism

The Holy Ghost

Ordinances

Covenants

Exaltation

Article 1st of Faith 1

Article 2nd of Faith 17

Article 3rd of Faith 34

Article 4th of Faith 50

Article 5th of Faith 75

Article 6th of Faith 91

Article 7th of Faith 107

Article 8th of Faith 130

Article 9th of Faith 146

Article 10th of Faith 161

Article 11th of Faith 177

Article 12th of Faith 193

Article 13th of Faith 209

About the Author 227

We believe in God, the Eternal Father, and in His Son, Jesus Christ, and in the Holy Ghost.

The Psalmist wrote about those who "reel to and fro, and stagger like a drunken man, and are at their wits' end." (Psalms 107:27). Daniel described his king, whose "thoughts troubled him, so that the joints of his loins were loosed, and his

knees smote one against another." (Daniel 5:6). When our faith is not grounded in the Father, Son, and Holy Ghost, the fibers of our being become uncoordinated, and we lose our physical, emotional, and especially our spiritual coherence.

Satan uses telestial toys, the corruptible treasures of the earth, as counterfeits for God. They are the polar opposites of celestial surety and the riches of eternity. Jeremiah asked the obvious question: "Shall a man make gods unto himself, and they are no gods?"

(Jeremiah 16:20). In the end, the seducer only rules by manipulating those who worship idols. His followers have traded their birthright of agency for a mess of pottage, surrendering it for the fleeting rush of carnality and sensuality he provides. But at what a great cost does it come!

Without a foundation that is firmly anchored on our Heavenly Father, His Son Jesus Christ, and the Holy Ghost, our central nervous system synaptic connections will only fire sporadically.

If we fail to utilize the principles of the Plan, we will respond to our environment inappropriately. Left to our own devices, our efforts will be ineffective and without synchronization.

Coast redwoods are among the largest living things. The tallest tree reaches a height of over 360 feet, weighs hundreds of tons, and has been alive for well over 2,000 years. But, curiously, while most other trees of massive size have deep roots to anchor their great weight, the root system of the redwood is very

shallow. The key to its survival is the inter-twining of the roots of one tree with those of several of its neighbors. Redwoods live in groves; they cannot stand alone. Interdependence is critical to the stability and longevity of each individual tree.

In the scriptures, those who were firm in the faith "came forth and caught hold of the end of the rod of iron; and they did press forward through the mist of darkness, clinging to the rod of iron, even until they did come forth and partake of the fruit of the tree." (1 Nephi 8:24). The rod of iron,

was a lightning rod, firmly grounding them to unchanging principles, that they might "henceforth be no more children, tossed to and fro," like flotsam and jetsam on the sea of life, "and carried about with every wind of doctrine." (Ephesians 4:14).

When we harden our hearts against the Lord, we "become like unto a flint." (2 Nephi 5:21). Then, when the inevitable sparks fly, hatred toward our fellow men bursts into flames that are fanned by the winds of intolerance and fueled by fear, prejudice, narrow-mindedness, and ignorance. The resulting fragility of

the pathways through which inspiration flows effectively cripples our capacity to respond to promptings of the Spirit. Conscious rejection of gospel principles propels the stubborn and headstrong on an accelerating spiral straight down into the gaping mouth of hell.

Sometimes, those who are not well-grounded need to be jolted out of their complacency, in the same way that defibrillator paddles are used to restore normal cardiac rhythm in those who have suffered heart failure. The

Savior's instruction to Nephi comes to mind: "Stretch forth thine hand again unto thy brethren, and...I will shock them, saith the Lord, and this will I do, that they may know that I am the Lord their God." (1 Nephi 17:53).

Heavenly Parents participated jointly in the creative process. In ways that others cannot fully appreciate, Latter-day Saints recognize their own responsibility to provide nurturing environments for the spirit children who have been entrusted

into their care. Father and mother have sacred roles, and are part of a grand Plan envisioned by God Himself to make sure that the family reaches its intended stature; and that is to become the basic building block of eternity.

It is not enough that we know about our Father and His Son by reading the Gospels, or by listening to others speak of Them. We must know Them through the bonds of common experience and feeling. After all, true religion is more involved with recovery than it is with

discovery. Our destiny is not just to enjoy union, but also a reunion with divine realities. Religious recognition is simply our re-acquaintance with the visions of eternity, or that which we learned during our pre-mortal spiritual childhood.

The Three Act Play is heaven's best gift to mankind. Its name is The Plan of Salvation. Whereas the most successful productions on Broadway close after only a few years, The Plan of Salvation

has been around since before our first parents attended opening night of the Second Act in the Garden in Eden. Its run will extend into the eternities, where the Third Act will engage the attention of its participants forever.

God, Who is the Author of Salvation and the Builder of the universe and all things therein, is able to read the blueprint of our lives with unerring accuracy. But in a sense, we are in a partnership with the Master Designer. Therefore, we should be

vigilant to see that we exercise our agency to engage in the building of a holy temple for the eternal dwelling place of our souls. Life was intended to be more than just an overnight stay in a cheap, 2nd class hotel room.

Seraphim describe the Lord of Hosts as "holy, holy, holy." This expression suggests to our minds temple attendants, who call to one another in a three-fold petition. Exodus 20:13 recounts the experience of Moses on Sinai, when the Lord spoke to him out of the burning bush: "And all

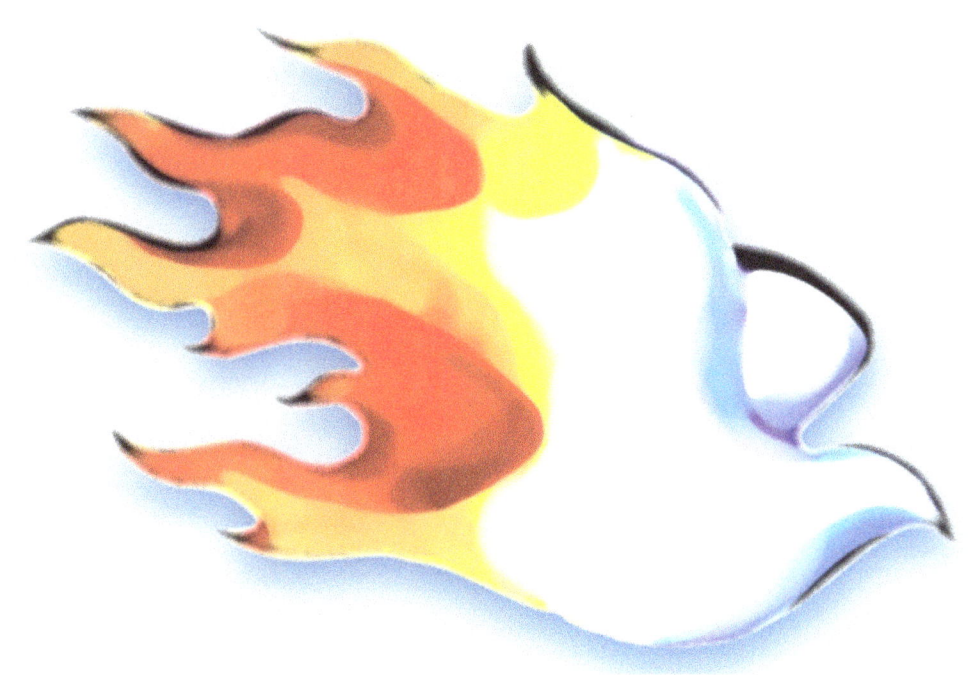

the people saw the thunderings, and the lightnings, and the noise of the trumpet, and the mountain smoking." The Doctrine & Covenants similarly describes the signs of the coming of the Son of Man: "They shall behold blood and fire, and vapors of smoke." (D&C 45:41).

Grace is an attribute of God that consists of the love, mercy, and power by which He may bring us to His stature. His grace allows us to enjoy not only what He has, but also what He is. On

earth, our lives are days of probation, of testing, or of putting to the proof our declared values. Therefore, as we commit to conform to His lifestyle, we may more fully grow in His grace.

When prayer to God is riddled with expressions of false doctrine, the seeds of apostasy take root. Some convey the sense that God is a spirit. Others suggest the veneration of Mary, or of saints. Such prayer can be sterile and devoid of

vitality. Offered by rote, it becomes impotent, and powerless. That many engage in such a stylistic ritual is astonishing to those who have become accustomed to more intimate levels of conversation with God.

The cancer of materialism chokes out our capacity to respond to spiritual promptings. Focusing on the work of the kingdom, however, helps us to maintain our perspective, while at the same time strengthening our reverence

for God's work. Indeed, the earth, sun, moon and stars "roll upon their wings in their glory....and any man who hath seen any or the least of these hath seen God moving in his majesty and power." (D&C 88:45-46).

We believe that men will be punished for their own sins, and not for Adam's transgression.

"Adam fell that men might be, and men are that they might have joy." (2 Nephi 2:25). When we consider the Fall in conjunction with the Atonement of Christ, it is clear that both are part of God's Plan of Eternal Progression for us and that its intended goal is our

happiness. Joseph Smith said: "Happiness is the object and design of our existence and will be the end thereof, if we pursue the path that leads to it; and this path is virtue, uprightness, faithfulness, holiness, and keeping all the commandments."

Satan "sought to beguile Eve, for he knew not the mind of God, wherefore he sought to destroy the world." (Moses 4:6). To counteract his efforts, a mighty change must be wrought in our hearts. We need to let the Atonement works its miracle, that we might have the spirit of prophecy, the testimony of Jesus, and a greater under-

standing of the mysteries of the kingdom. We are born again, not by maturation, but instead by generation. We become "new creature(s): old things are passed away; behold, all things are become new." (2 Corinthians 5:7). His forgiveness allows us to be "void of offense towards God, and towards all men." (D&C 135:5).

When Adam and Eve were driven from the Garden, they were "punished" with the very things that would later prove to bring them the greatest happiness. Cherubim and a flaming sword were placed to keep the way of the tree of life, to preserve the principles of the Plan of Salvation in the presence of

the powerful influence of moral agency that Adam and Eve now enjoyed. Both justice and mercy were brought into balance through the Atonement, that they and their posterity might enjoy the wonders of mortality, without jeopardizing their eternal identity.

Danger lies in a comfortable awareness of sin. As Alexander Pope observed: "Vice is a monster of such frightful

mein, as to be hated needs but to be seen. Yet seen too oft, familiar with her face, we first pity, then endure, then embrace."

After the Fall, the door to Eden may have swung shut, but there was opened to us another portal leading to the knowledge of both good and evil, in the wonderful learning laboratory of mortality. The Plan was designed to transform our nature with the transplant

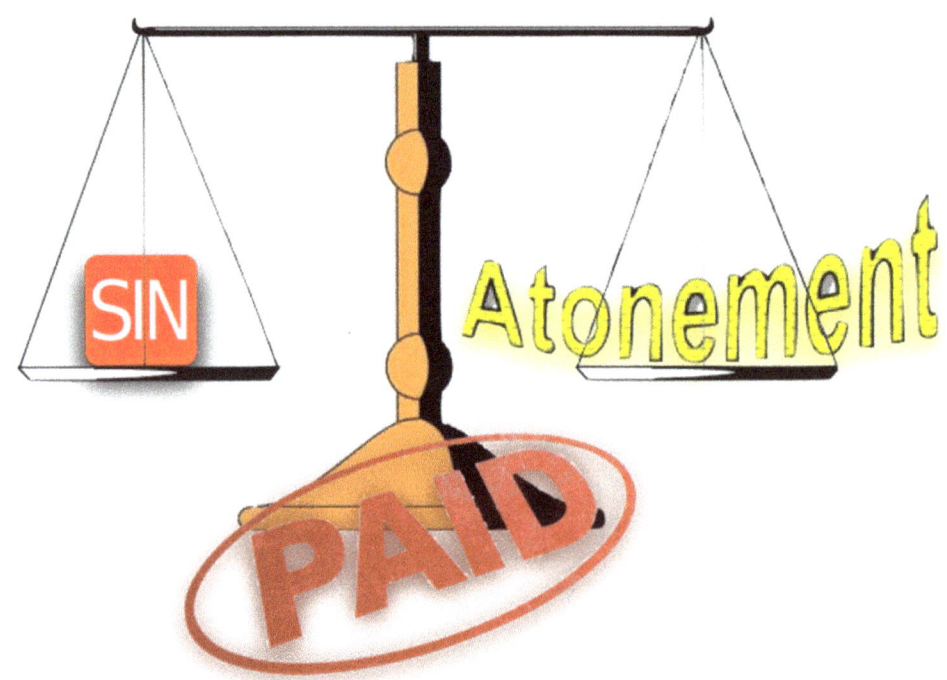

of a new heart, that we might become spiritually aerobically fit, and reach our potential in the image and likeness of God. The world seeks change from the outside, and fails miserably. The gospel changes us, and our hearts, from the inside, and succeeds brilliantly.

"All those who humble themselves before God, and desire to be baptized, and come forth with broken hearts and contrite spirits, and witness before the church that they have truly repented of all their sins, and are willing to take upon them the name of Jesus Christ,

having a determination to serve him to the end, and truly manifest by their works that they have received the Spirit of Christ unto the remission of their sins, shall be received by baptism into his church." (D&C 20:37).

To truly appreciate the value of our lives, we need to journey in our mind's eye back to a land before time, during the creative period when matter was organized, the elements were brought out of chaos into order, and a Garden

was created in a place that was called Eden. We need to remember that when God had finished His work, He saw that it was "very good." (Genesis 1:31).

Death is as much a part of life as is birth, and Adam's transgression was integral to the execution of the Plan, inasmuch as it gave us the opportunity to be born into this world, to live, and to die. When it was finally our time to

come to earth, others smiled at our birth, while we cried. When our time comes to leave, our loved ones will cry, while we will smile. Only then will we realize that death is only a comma, and not the exclamation point that it seemed to be.

Everything was as the Architect of the Plan had imagined it would be. Each detail had been pre-played in eternity before it was re-played in the vast expanse of the temporal cosmos. There were no costly change orders. The

storyboard had first been created spiritually, and only then physically. As God explained: "By the power of my Spirit created I...all things both spiritual and temporal. First spiritual, secondly temporal." (D&C 29:31-32).

In music, David expressed his hope in the universality of the Atonement: "Thou wilt not leave my soul in hell." He exclaimed. "Thou wilt shew me the path of life. In thy presence is fulness of joy; at thy right hand there are pleasures for evermore." (Psalms 16:10-11). Later,

the Lord explained to Joseph Smith: "Verily I say unto you, all among them who know their hearts are honest, and are broken, and their spirits contrite, and are willing to observe their covenants by sacrifice — yea, every sacrifice which I, the Lord, shall command — they are accepted of me." (D&C 97:8).

In a Garden setting, we do not think of our first parents' violation of law as sin, for they did not have moral agency when they made their choice. Mortality was not a punishment, but rather the inevitable consequence of the transgression of law. It was more like a mechanical infraction than a moving violation. In the light of

latter-day revelation that explains in greater detail what transpired in the Garden before and after the Fall, it would seem that Mercy and Justice were applied with special provisos, caveats, codicils, and addenda that were unique at the time, but that now generally apply to all of God's children.

Adam's later experiences as a result of the Fall are shining examples of spiritual maturation in the light of day. In the face of opposition, he would keep the commandments with exactness. God's confidence in his capacity to carry out his responsibilities as they related

to the Plan would be validated. "And after many days an angel of the Lord appeared unto Adam, saying: Why dost thou offer sacrifices unto the Lord? And Adam said unto him: I know not, save the Lord commanded me." (Moses 5:6).

The doctrine of Christ is to have faith, repent of sin, enter into a baptismal covenant, and then receive the Holy Ghost, Who will direct our development, revealing the things we must do to merit salvation. "For the gate by which (we) should enter is repentance and baptism

by water; and then," in a mystical and incomprehensible way, there comes "a remission of (our) sins by fire and by the Holy Ghost." This puts us squarely on the "strait and narrow path which leads to eternal life" through God's matchless grace. (2 Nephi 31:17-18).

Those who fight against Zion are wicked and adulterous in the sense that they have fornicated with the seducer by being unfaithful to gospel principles. Both individuals and institutions are corrupt and promiscuous when idols have become the focus of their worship. Those who are

not with God are against Him. Ezekiel wrote that those who allow themselves to be led into spiritual bondage, become "as the heathen, as the families of the countries, to serve (powerless idols of) wood and stone." (Ezekiel 20:32).

Members of Christ's church have a moral responsibility to teach the true points of His doctrine, in order that the gospel might be established among the nations, that all might receive the ordinances of salvation and be released from the awful burden of sin. Those who twist the scriptures, by wresting them from

their proper signification, pervert them from their correct application. Such is the case when individuals alter their meaning to justify damnable doctrines; for example, that little children, who are redeemed in Christ, need baptism.

In our day, Babylon has become entrenched in the world and is "the great whore that sitteth upon many waters, with whom the kings of the earth have committed fornication." (Revelation 17:1-2). In the eyes of

the Lord, all of the profane governments of the earth have prostituted themselves by becoming corrupt institutions that no longer trust in God or believe that they live and move and have their being under His divine provenance.

We believe that through the Atonement of Christ, all mankind may be saved, by obedience to the laws and ordinances of the gospel.

"Come unto Christ, and lay hold upon every good gift, and touch not the evil gift, nor the unclean thing. Yea, come

unto Christ, and be perfected in him, and deny yourselves of all ungodliness." (Moroni 10:30 & 32).

Our own maturation traces the pattern established by the Savior, Whose work followed a natural progression and was built line upon line and precept upon precept until His preparation was complete and every necessary detail had been

worked out. Early in His ministry, Jesus had said, "My time is not yet come." (John 7:6). But later, when all had been accomplished, He confirmed, "My time is at hand." (Matthew 26:18).

Today, the crucified Christ is the primary focus of Christianity, but if we fail to understand the Mortal Messiah, we risk receiving only a one-dimensional view that ignores the wonderful harmony of His humanity with His divinity. Those who

have known hardship, as He did, are usually much better able to help others to deal with their own adversity. This may help to explain why so many church members, even after living Christ-like lives, are not spared such challenges.

"If ye by the grace of God are perfect in Christ, and deny not his power, then are ye sanctified in Christ by the grace of God, through the shedding of the blood of Christ, which is in the covenant of the Father unto the remission of your sins, that ye become holy, without spot." (Moroni 10:33). It would be difficult for

the essence of the gospel be put more succinctly, yet more powerfully, than in this verse. We can become even as Jesus, Who was as a lamb without spot or blemish. Through His Atonement, we can be "perfect, even as (our) Father which is in Heaven is perfect." Matthew 5:48).

It would be wrong to assume that the more righteous we are, the less we will suffer. His promise is that we will be blessed, even though our blessing may simply be the strength to endure our

trials. All suffer. The difference is that the wicked must suffer the consequences of sin, in addition to the suffering that is a necessary part of our experience.

Jesus said to the woman at the well: "Whosoever drinketh of this water shall thirst again: But whosoever drinketh of the water that I shall give him shall never thirst; but the water that I shall

give him shall be in him a well of water springing up into everlasting life." John 4:10-14). The living water that sustains us spiritually is the doctrine of the gospel of Jesus Christ.

"We talk of Christ, we rejoice in Christ, we preach of Christ, we prophesy of Christ, and we write according to our prophecies, that our children may know to what source they may look for a remission of their sins." (2 Nephi 25:26).

We have learned to love Him, just as we have learned that blessings will follow obedience. The principles of the gospel do not change over time, nor do the requirements for obtaining salvation. They are the same for all of His children.

The Saints of all ages know how the people of Zarahemla must have felt when they exclaimed to Benjamin: "We believe all the words which thou hast spoken unto us; and also, we know of their surety and truth, because of the

Spirit of the Lord Omnipotent, which has wrought a mighty change in us, or in our hearts, that we have no more disposition to do evil, but to do good continually." (Mosiah 5:2).

As the morning breaks over the eastern sky, and the sunrise heralds another day, we once again address the self-evident truth. We have been born again. We have

met the challenges before us, and with gratitude, have received our new hearts. Reinvigorated with energy, we recommit ourselves completely to His service.

Critics might see only frivolous repetition in our efforts to maintain spiritually aerobic health, mistaking our spiritual focus for detachment from an active lifestyle that concentrates on physical fitness as an end in itself. But sooner or

later, there is for each of us who has had a spiritual heart transplant a moment in the sun, when the light of understanding illuminates our mind and confirms the divine potential of the new organ that beats steadily in our chest.

Our new hearts provide the spiritual element that is necessary to sustain our forward momentum as we push on into the unexplored reaches of eternity. We realize that our new hearts are both a physiological and spiritual improvement.

They have been designed not only to improve our lifestyle, but also to sustain life itself. With all diligence, we exercise our new hearts to their potential, to keep them vital and healthy, knowing that it is from them that the fundamental issues of life will flow as a revelatory stream.

We make sacred covenants with the Lord, the fulfillment of which may bring us earthly comforts but will surely bless us with eternal exaltation. As we focus

our attention on our love of the Lord and our obedience to His instruction, our thirst is quenched by the fountain of living water that has been provided by the gospel of Jesus Christ.

Just as we are known by the name of our mortal parents, so too are we called by the name of Christ, in a familial way. We are His children in the sense that He saved our souls through the Atonement, and united our bodies and spirits through

the Resurrection. "For this day He hath spiritually begotten you," explained King Benjamin. (Mosiah 5:7). When we have come to that epiphany, we will appreciate the special relationship that has been reserved for the faithful, that is in addition to our understanding that we are all spirit children of our Father.

Although we now reside in the midst of spiritual Babylon, we keep our covenants so that we can live with confidence and high hopes for the future. We can be the happiest people on the face of the earth. In 1830, the Lord declared: "The day

speedily cometh; the hour is not yet, but is nigh at hand, when peace shall be taken from the earth, and the devil shall have power over his own dominion." (D&C 1:35). "But if (we) are prepared, (we) shall not fear." (D&C 38:30).

Keeping covenants puts us beyond the power of the adversary and blesses us with the perspective to overcome evil and obtain exaltation. The Prophet Joseph Smith said that salvation consists of our being placed beyond

the power of our enemies, meaning the enemies of our progression, such as dishonesty, greediness, lying, immorality, and other vices. These are the very character flaws that our covenants give us the power to overcome.

Article 4th of Faith

We believe that the first principles and ordinances of the gospel are: first, Faith in the Lord Jesus Christ; second, Repentance; third, Baptism by immersion for the remission of sins; fourth, Laying on of hands for the gift of the Holy Ghost.

Authority empowers church leaders to administer the first principles and ordinances of salvation. Just as they did in former times, those who hold the priesthood today teach the two fundamental principles of faith and

repentance, and then, perform the two basic ordinances of baptism and receipt of the Holy Ghost. As the Savior taught: Except we be born of water and of the Spirit, we "cannot enter into the kingdom of God." (John 3:5).

The gift of faith motivates us to action. The miracles from the Standard Works with which we are familiar were only made possible by the exercise of faith, and each of us has the power to develop a testimony of principles with the same

intensity of feeling. When we read in the scriptural accounts of these experiences, we realize that Heavenly Father has prepared a way for us to be partakers of the same heavenly gifts.

The Holy Ghost impresses upon us the powerful feeling experienced by the two disciples on the Road to Emmaus, who, after communing with the resurrected

Lord, declared: "Did not our heart burn within us while he talked with us by the way, and while he opened to us the scriptures?" (Luke 24:32).

"Though your sins be as scarlet, they shall be as white as snow; though they be red like crimson, they shall be as wool." (Isaiah 1:18). When the gospel drives the law into our inward parts, so that it is written upon our hearts, a mighty change takes place as we

experience the process of sanctification. When we are born again, we have no more disposition to do evil. Our "minds become single to God, and" the promise is given that "the days will come that (we) shall see him; for he will unveil his face unto (us)." (D&C 88:68).

On the Day of Pentecost, over three thousand people "were pricked in their heart, and said unto Peter and to the rest of the apostles, men and brethren, what shall we do? Then Peter said unto them.

repent, and be baptized every one of you in the name of Jesus Christ for the remission of sins, and ye shall receive the gift of the Holy Ghost." (Acts 2:37-38).

The Plan helps us to internalize gospel principles through sanctification by the Spirit. It provides the covenants and ordinances that will enable us to live once again in a state of holiness in the presence of our Father. It cleanses us in a spiritual renewal that prepares us to pass by the angels who stand as sentinels

as we approach the veil, ready to enter the presence of the Lord. It provides a way for us to submit to His will and yield our hearts to Him, by obedience to the teachings of His church. By doing these things, we are confident that we "shall be lifted up at the last day." (3 Nephi 27:22).

"Now I say unto you, if this be the desire of your hearts, what have you against being baptized in the name of the Lord, as a witness before him that ye have

entered into a covenant with him, that ye will serve him and keep his commandments, that he may pour out his Spirit more abundantly upon you?" (Mosiah 18:10).

As we tarry on earth, ordinances expose us to a multitude of spiritual gifts that allow us to walk in the light of truth. Paul told the Corinthian saints: "Now there are diversities of gifts." (1 Corinthians 12:4). With these gifts, the image of God is engraven upon our countenances. "Who shall ascend into the hill of the Lord,"

asked the Psalmist, "or who shall stand in his holy place" to partake of the Divine Nature? "He that hath clean hands and a pure heart; who" is a partaker of wonderful spiritual gifts, and "hath not lifted up his soul unto vanity, nor sworn deceitfully." (Psalms 24:4-5).

"And they continued steadfastly in the apostles' doctrine and fellowship, and in breaking of bread, and in prayers." (Acts 2:42). The ordinances of salvation propelled them along on a pathway of

progression that would lead them to exaltation in the kingdom of God. The "bread and wine" of which they partook in the ordinance of the Sacrament, were "the emblems of the flesh and blood of Christ." (D&C 20:40).

Christ is the Author of Salvation and the Finisher of our Faith, but the Plan itself was introduced to His spirit children by Heavenly Father. The Holy Ghost testifies of Christ and of the Father by the spirit

of revelation. In perfect harmony, the three members of the Godhead promote the doctrine of Christ with one shared goal: To bring us to the waters of baptism, whose gentle currents lap upon the shoreline of the Celestial Kingdom.

The Holy Ghost is a fountain of facts and figures, a storehouse of knowledge, a lifetime of learning, a repository of reassurance, a spring of sagacity, a talisman of talents, and a warehouse of wisdom. He is the author of acumen, the avatar of agency, the architect of aptitude, the benefactor of blessings,

the champion of committed Christians, the craftsman of comfort, the designer of our discipleship, the engineer of erudition, the guarantor of gifts, the initiator of insight, the inventor of intelligence, the patron of perception, the provider of providence, the sponsor of scholarship, and the ultimate source of our understanding of the eternities.

The Holy Ghost testifies of truth and is the aether within which we communicate with our Heavenly Father. He makes our lives complete. Links that are forged by the Holy Ghost create an unbreakable

relationship with God. He is the mortar securing us to the Chief Corner Stone. He defines the bounds and the conditions that define how we can emulate our Father and discover for ourselves His nature and reflect His holy attributes.

It is worth becoming familiar with the Holy Ghost, "getting to know all about Him, getting to like Him, and getting to hope He like us. Putting it another way, but nicely, He is precisely our cup of tea, getting to feel free and easy when we

are with Him. Haven't you noticed that suddenly we're bright and breezy, because of all the beautiful and new things we're learning about Him day by day." (Adapted from "The King and I," "Getting to Know You," lyrics by Lorenz Hart and Richard Rodgers).

When, at last, we come back into the presence of God our Father, it will be through the tender mercies, loving guidance, concerned supervision, the nurturing influence, dizzying inspiration, and powerful witness of the Holy Ghost.

His spirit will authoritatively justify us before the throne of God. It will be according to His unimpeachable testimony that we will be weighed in the balances and will be measured.

The Holy Ghost is our obstetrical specialist as we are born again and become new creatures in Christ. He is our gerontologist who will mitigate the culture shock when we make the inevitable transition from telestial trappings to our heavenly home. He

is the figurative counterpart to tangible elements, for except we "be born of water and of the spirit," we cannot "enter into the kingdom of God." (John 3:5). He is the third member of the Godhead, and it is only through His sustaining support that we enjoy spiritual life.

We make initial preparations to take up eventual residence in the mansions that have been prepared for us by submitting ourselves to baptism by water. But that demonstration of faith and obedience only unlatches and nudges open the

portal leading to the Celestial Kingdom. "For the gate by which ye should enter is repentance and baptism by water; and" only "then cometh a remission of your sins by fire and by the Holy Ghost." (2 Nephi 31:17).

The Plan of Salvation cannot operate to our benefit without discernment. Were it not for the gift of the Holy Ghost, the Plan would be crippled and work to our

detriment and even to our damnation. Its finest features would be thrown into turmoil without the moral element of responsibility that is so tenderly provided by the Holy Ghost.

When we view the supernal gift of the Holy Ghost as an endowment of spiritual and priesthood power, we can see that only those who have engaged the saving ordinances of the gospel, and have

embarked upon a path leading to exaltation in the Celestial Kingdom, unleash healing at the level and intensity that is quietly provided by intimate association with the third member of the Godhead.

Our God-given senses cannot replace the influence of the Spirit. "The wind bloweth where it listeth, and thou hearest the sound thereof, but canst not tell whence it cometh, and whither it goeth: so is every one that is born of the Spirit." (John 3:8). If we use our physical

senses to excess, relying on our intellect and instinct while ignoring spiritual promptings that are provided in a rarified atmosphere like a refreshing breeze on a hot summer day, we will fall short of our promised perception potential provided by the providential pattern of the Plan.

If we do not know, or choose to ignore the Holy Ghost, we become susceptible to three dangers. The first is indifference, or a lack of commitment. If we do not know the Master, how can we be expected to serve Him with all our heart, might, mind, and strength? The second is waywardness, or straying from gospel standards. If we are unprincipled and

we believe in nothing, how can we be expected to stand for anything? The third is rebellion, or active opposition to the principles of truth. If the light is extinguished, how can we avoid stumbling over hidden obstacles in the gathering gloom?

King Benjamin cautioned his people: "This much I can tell you, that if ye do not watch yourselves, and your thoughts, and your words, and your deeds, and observe the commandments of God, and continue

in the faith of what ye have heard concerning the coming of our Lord, even unto the end of your lives, ye must perish." (Mosiah 4:30).

"By the power of the Spirit, our eyes (are) opened and our understanding (is) enlightened, so as to see and understand the things of God." (D&C 76:12). The Savior helps us to forget our bad days and to focus on

becoming better; to be more responsible towards others, and to help them, to sacrifice ourselves through His love, and to be willing participants in the creation of a bit of heaven on earth, as we assist others on their journey to Christ.

When we partake of the Sacrament, we can almost smell the sweet fragrance of celestial gardens, and we hear the Spirit speak "of things as they really are, and of things as they really will be," as these truths are "manifested unto us plainly, for the salvation of our souls." (Jacob

4:13). We hear a voice whispering: "Well done thou good and faithful servant. Enter thou into the joy of the Lord." (Matthew 25:21). We are propelled back into the presence of God in a spiritual transformation, through the nurturing influence of the Holy Ghost.

The Holy Ghost eliminates ambiguity in our lives by clarifying the elements of the Plan. It brings accountability into sharp focus, and provides us with an orientation that is squarely fixed on the Celestial Kingdom. Positive outcomes

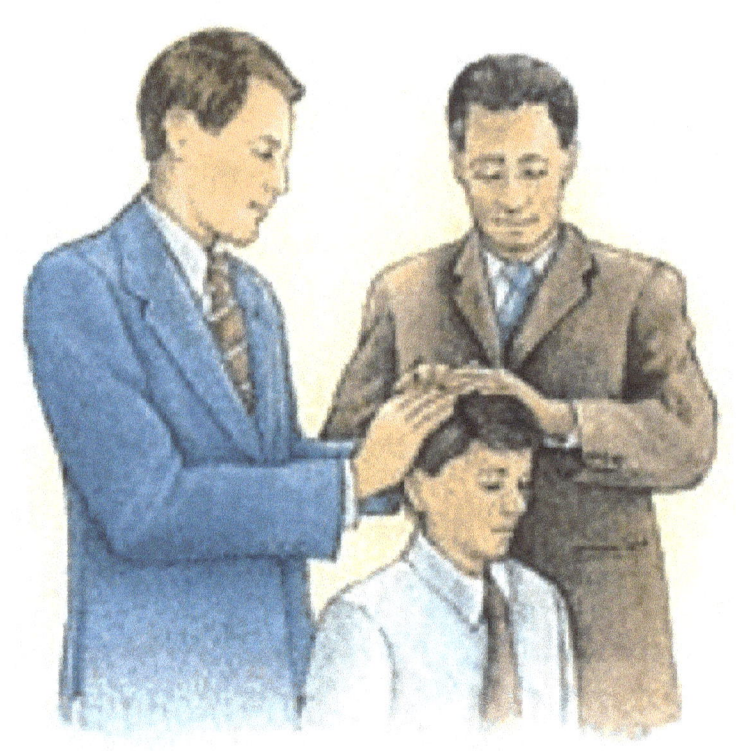

are promised and provided by the Plan, and are woven into covenants that allow us to actively express our love, and that at the same time, reinforce our power to act autonomously. It is in this way that we are able to stand independent above all creatures.

Article 5th of Faith

We believe that a man must be called of God, by prophecy, and by the laying on of hands by those who are in authority, to preach the Gospel and administer in the ordinances thereof.

The Lord has created a wonderful program designed to bring family exaltation within reach of all of His children.

It is called "Sharing the Gospel." But missionary work is not easy, because, as Dallin Oaks observed, it turns out that "salvation is not a cheap experience."

All who "have desires to serve God" are called to the work. (D&C 4:3). Our most important mission in life is to keep the commandments and to teach them to others of our Father in Heaven's children. As we who are enlisted in the missionary

army of Jesus Christ continue to focus our attention on our brothers and sisters who have not yet received the gospel, they too will be brought into complete harmony with the nature of the Father of our spirits, and they will be alive in Jesus Christ.

Spencer W. Kimball taught: "We have paused on some plateaus long enough. Let us resume our journey forward and upward, and quietly put an end to our reluctance to reach out to others,

whether in our own families, wards, or neighborhoods. We have been diverted at times from fundamentals on which we must now focus, in order to move forward as a person or as a people."

Professors of religion often "teach for doctrines the commandments of men, having a form of godliness, but they deny the power thereof." (J.S.H. 1:19). Creeds are an abomination in the sight of God, and are corrupt, when they

lead His children away from the truth. Insult is added to injury when hypocrisy further perverts humanized, spiritually impotent dogma, when people do not really believe, but are only "professors" of religion.

Gordon B. Hinckley declared: "The church cannot hope to save a man on Sunday, if during the week it is a complacent witness to the destruction of his soul." Rather

than only occasionally taking glowing embers out into the world, we need to bring others into the roaring fire of the gospel, the church, and the kingdom.

When God said: "Let us make man in our image, after our likeness," He meant not only that we would have the same physical appearance as our Parents, but also that we would enjoy their spiritual characteristics, as well. (Moses 2:26). When we are finally "like" Him, it will

be because we have matured to reach the full stature of our spirits and have nurtured the god in embryo that lies undiscovered within us. The magic of the gospel is its power to touch us and vitalize that divine potential, in the miracle of our spiritual rebirth.

David O McKay spoke of the personal interview each of us will one day have with the Savior. "He will want a summary of your activity in your church assignments. He will not necessarily be interested in

what assignments you have had, for in His eyes, the home teacher and a mission president are probably equals, but he will request a summary of how you have been of service to your fellow man."

Priesthood authority is our secret weapon in the ideological war that is being waged with Satan. It bursts the fetters that bind us to sin and threaten to drag us down to hell. In some cases, it may be

our only defense against the insidious influence of moral equivocation. When we find ourselves standing alone against the world, and the rule of law falls far below the gospel standard, authority creates an impenetrable shield of invincibility.

We can be missionaries by teaching correct principles, and by trying to be good examples. If we are undeviatingly true to ourselves, we can be false to no man. Maybe missionary work need be

no more complicated than loving others as we love ourselves. We do missionary work because we love God's children. If we learn to love as He does, and live to learn, we'll love to live, and our charity will be infectious.

The amazing thing about priesthood authority is that when those who have it exercise its power, the manner in which others within auxiliary organizations

serve is influenced with spectacular results. In addition, we can be sure that the united voice of those who hold the keys of the kingdom will always unerringly govern the church and strengthen its members.

The Lord does not need our help to defend His kingdom. Yet there are those who fear the ark is teetering precariously and would presume to steady it. Their best intentions, however, do not justify interference with the Lord's Plan. See how quickly those who attempt to steady the ark die spiritually. Such is the pitiable condition of those who, neglecting their own responsibilities, spend their time in

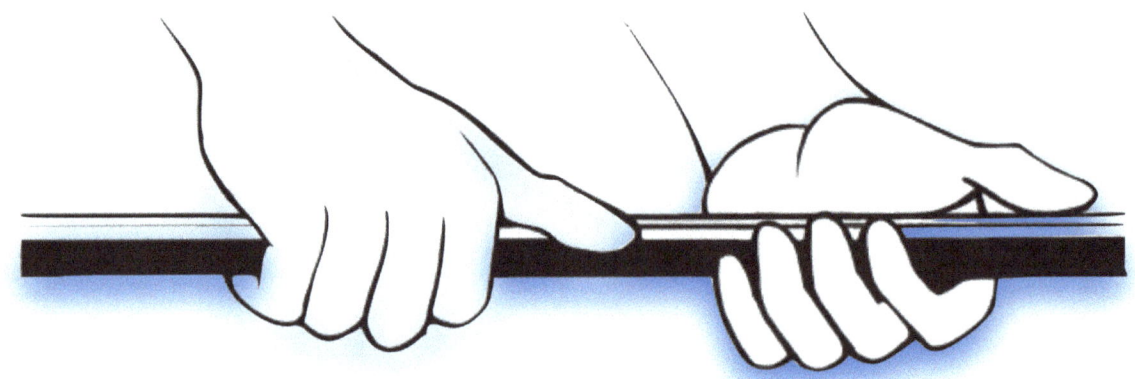

finding fault with the management of the Lord's kingdom. The ark does not need steadying, especially by those with neither ability nor authority, and without revelation or knowledge of the laws that govern Zion. We need to look to our leaders for our instruction, adhere to correct principles, and remain faithful.

Anciently, the prophets repeatedly warned Israel against dalliances with magicians, sorcerers, witches, astrologers, familiar spirits, exorcists, and participation in divinations, enchantments, and other

activities that encourage or solicit the intervention of evil spirits. These temptations may have undergone a facelift, but their underlying menace remains unchanged.

Paul taught that the key to gospel knowledge is personal revelation. He said: "Let him be accursed who preaches any other gospel." (Galatians 1:8-12). "That which is of God is light; and he that receiveth light, and continueth in

God, receiveth more light; and that light groweth brighter and brighter until the perfect day." (D&C 50:24). Who could hope for more pointed instruction than that which is given in this simple counsel?

The gospel of Jesus Christ is "The Good News" to those who embrace it, because it encompasses all the principles, covenants, and ordinances that enable us to become sanctified so that we may be worthy to live once again in a state of holiness in the

presence of our Heavenly Father. His grace makes it possible to "come unto Christ, and lay hold upon every good gift...and (to) be perfected in him," as we eschew "all ungodliness." (Moroni 10:30 & 32).

Sanctification is the process by which we so profoundly rely upon the merits of Christ and His Atonement that we are cleansed from the effects of sin. Thus spiritually renewed, we receive health in our navels and marrow in our bones, and

we stand prepared to enter His presence. We submit to His will, yield our hearts to Him, sustain His servants, preach His gospel, participate in His ordinances, enter into His covenants, and are obedient to all of the teachings of His church.

We believe in the same organization that existed in the Primitive Church, namely, apostles, prophets, pastors, teachers, evangelists, and so forth.

For some reason, the inherent structure of the church is not obvious to Christians of other faiths. They don't see things as we do. And yet, the Pope himself stated the obvious: "Even the humblest human

beings are naturally philosophic," he observed, "asking themselves 'Who am I?' 'Where do I come from?' and 'Where am I going?' Religious revelation provides answers to these questions," the pope acknowledged." (John Paul II).

Jesus Christ established a church compared by Paul to a structure that was "built upon the foundation of the apostles and prophets, Jesus Christ himself being the chief corner stone." (Ephesians 2:20). Accordingly, "he gave some, apostles; and some, prophets, and some, evangelists; and some, pastors

and teachers; For the perfecting of the saints, for the work of the ministry, for the edifying of the body of Christ: Till we all come in the unity of the faith, and of the knowledge of the Son of God, unto a perfect man, unto the measure of the stature of the fulness of Christ." (Ephesians 4:11-13).

Jesus foresaw the need for priesthood leaders to assist the Apostles in the work of the ministry. In pairs, He sent officers called Seventies to preach the gospel. Others were evangelists (patriarchs), pastors (presiding leaders), high priests,

elders, bishops, priests, teachers, and deacons. These servants of the Lord provided missionary work, performed ordinances, and instructed and inspired church members to come to a unity of the faith, and of the knowledge of the Son of God.

The Lord numbers His children by their willingness to accept covenants, and His missionary objective is quite simple. Just find those who are the elect, and let the Spirit introduce them to the gospel. "And ye are called to bring to pass the gathering of mine elect," declared the Lord, "for mine elect hear my voice

and harden not their hearts." (D&C 29:7). We cannot follow our own agenda or anchor our own values to the shifting sands of expediency, rather than on the principles that are the bedrock of the doctrine of Christ. We must not take strength unto ourselves, or try to bring the world into the gospel, instead of taking the gospel into the world.

Religion becomes "magical," when the power by which the clergy operates is transferred from God to those who profess to be His earthly representatives, but who are really only competing for "market share." The Bible, under these circumstances, conveys knowledge

without the aid of revelation. Beware those who bear the priesthood, if it has acquired the status of an office that automatically bestows power and grace without regard for the moral or spiritual qualifications of its possessor.

"For behold, the field is white already to harvest; and it is the eleventh hour, and the last time that I shall call laborers into my vineyard." (D&C 33:3). Our lesson from the Parable of the Laborers in the Vineyard is that by continuing to focus

our attention on our brothers and sisters, our nature can be brought into harmony with the attributes of our Father in Heaven. "And ye shall be even as I am, and I am even as the Father, and the Father and I are one," said the Savior. (3 Nephi 28:10).

With the authority, of the priesthood, the primitive church administered the first principles and ordinances. Truth seekers were first taught to have faith, then to repent, and finally to

submit to baptism, that they might receive the Holy Ghost. As the Savior said: "Except a man be born of water and of the Spirit, he cannot enter into the kingdom of God." (John 3:5).

The Restoration burst upon the world in the wasteland of apostasy. Out of that wilderness will be gathered "the elect, even as many as will believe in (Him) and hearken unto (His) voice." (D&C 33:6). The gospel is preached because

the world needs to find its roots in foundation covenants. The message is proclaimed, not that people might enjoy a better life, but that God's children might be saved in His Celestial Kingdom.

During the Lord's ministry among the Nephites, He defined with greater clarity the name of His church, teaching: "If it be called in my name, then it is my church," with the qualifier that its foundation be "built upon my gospel." (3 Nephi 27:8).

Today, there are many organizations that have the name of Christ or a derivative in their titles, and so the substantive element that identifies the true church is its adherence to gospel principles that are taught by the His disciples.

Satan tries to defeat us by reducing our distinctive personality signatures to the lowest common denominator, thereby neutralizing our inventiveness, initiative, imagination, resourcefulness, and creativity, If we surrender these traits

that make us unique, we will fade into a shadow and a caricature of what we might have otherwise been. One of the greatest evidences of our individuality is our collective participation in the programs of the church and kingdom.

Joseph Fielding Smith. taught: "Before you joined the church you sat on neutral ground. When the gospel was preached, good and evil were set before you. You could choose either or neither. There were two opposite masters inviting you

to serve them. You left the neutral ground and you can never get back on to it. Should you forsake the Master you have enlisted to serve, it will be by the instigation of the evil one, and you will follow his dictation and be his servant."

One reason why our Father's Plan is perfect is that it is designed to provide us with positive feedback that we might correct our course. Its participants are strengthened by self-diagnostic tests

that are administered as frequently as needed, so that damaging data may be immediately identified and deleted. In this way, His Plan continually offers gentle suggestions for improvement.

Joseph Smith declared: "I teach people correct principles and they govern themselves." This is not the course of safety, but it is the best way for us to progress as fast as our desire will allow. God declared to Adam in the Garden of Eden: "Nevertheless, thou mayest choose for thyself, for it is

given unto thee." (Moses 3:17). In the church, we are taught how to use our agency to do what is right, and when this pattern is entrenched, our celestial character stands out sharply against the drab backdrop of mediocrity that is so prevalent in the world.

The reality of the apostasy and the subsequent restoration of priesthood authority was foretold in the scriptures, documented by secular history, and confirmed in the records of the church. "Of other churches, we do not say they

are wrong, so much as we say they are incomplete." (Boyd K. Packer). Today, The Church of Jesus Christ of Latter-day Saints has the full and unabridged support of "the only living and true God." (D&C 20:19).

The Church of Christ is one of the great signs of the times. But the world cannot see it, because it desires proof without the requisite exercise of faith. Only by doing our duty will our faith increase

until it becomes perfect knowledge. By faith, we believe what we do not see, but its reward is to see what we believe. So it is with signs from heaven. Under proper circumstances, signs can be empowering and boost the vitality of our faith.

We believe in the gift of tongues, prophecy, revelation, visions, healing, interpretation of tongues, and so forth.

Spiritual gifts were created "for the benefit of the children of God." (D&C 46:26). It will be difficult for those who have lived according to telestial law to justify their actions before God, in light of the many signs and wonders He has provided that reveal celestial sureties. Those "who hath

seen any or the least of these, hath seen God moving in his majesty and power." (D&C 88:47). Earth itself "is crammed with heaven, and every common bush with fire of God. But only those who see, take off their shoes. The rest stand around picking blackberries." (E.B. Browning).

The whisperings of the Spirit confirm to our hearts that there is more to the gospel than outward observances.

Spiritual enlightenment is the key to our discovery of undreamed of vistas of otherwise inaccessible experience.

Spiritual gifts illustrate the principles in which "the power of godliness is manifest. And without" the driving force of the affirmative actions behind these principles, "the power of godliness is not manifest unto men in the flesh. For without this,

no man can see the face of God, even the Father, and live." (D&C 84:20-22). The energy that animates the church in the latter days speaks for itself, and is a seamless continuation of the vitality that formerly quickened the church.

"Now there are diversities of gifts, but the same Spirit. ...But the manifestation of the Spirit is given to every man to profit withal. For to one is given by the Spirit the word of wisdom; to another the word of knowledge by the same Spirit; to another faith by

the same Spirit; to another the gifts of healing by the same Spirit; to another the working of miracles; to another prophecy; to another discerning of spirits; to another divers kinds of tongues; to another the interpretation of tongues." (1 Corinthians 12:4, 7-10).

Alma asked: "Have ye spiritually been born of God?" (Alma 5:14). He wanted to know if his brothers and sisters, who were baptized members of the church, had experienced the pure

and unconditional love of Christ, and if they had charity. He knew they had been converted to the church, but what he really wanted to find out was if they had also been converted to the gospel.

"All things must be done in the name of Christ, whatsoever you do in the Spirit." (D&C 46:31). Baptism qualifies us for membership in the church but does not assure the total spiritual transformation that is necessary to regain the presence of God. This

comes through the baptism of fire and the Holy Ghost, which is the receipt of the Spirit unto sanctification. "For by the water ye keep the commandment; by the Spirit ye are justified, and by the blood ye are sanctified." (Moses 6:60).

Mahatma Gandhi once said: "If a single man achieves the highest kind of love, it will be enough to neutralize the hatred of millions." The pure love of Christ in

our hearts is a dynamic influence for good. With this kind of dedication, we will be able to perform mighty miracles in His name, through the workings of the Spirit.

Every member of the church "is given a gift by the Spirit of God." (D&C 46:11). When these gifts find expression, they are positive, motivational, and uplifting. This

manifestation of spiritual gifts allows us to vividly pre-play, role-play, and re-play, that our agency might more comfortably find expression.

Every member of the church is invited to learn to understand the language of the Spirit with perfect fluency, for all too often we "tend to fill space, as if what we have, what we are, is not enough. Being affluent, we strangle ourselves with what

we can buy, things whose opacity obstructs our ability to see what is (really) there." (Gretel Erlich). Heavenly Father bestows upon us spiritual gifts, for He knows they are the antidote to the poisonous telestial tendencies that are the tares that would otherwise choke out the expression of celestial certainties.

"To some is given one (gift), and to some is given another, that all may be profited thereby." (D&C 46:12). At times, it is necessary to fast and pray to gain a witness of the Spirit, that we might receive a strong and independent

testimony of the gospel. It is only after we have paid the requisite price that we will be able to comprehend with fluency the poetic language of the Spirit. Otherwise, it will remain foreign to us.

If we have never made the journey to Christ, if we have not traveled the path leading to the tree of life, if we have not partaken of its delicious fruit, if we disregard the essentials, we cannot

receive "the things of the Spirit of God, for they are foolishness unto (us), neither can (we) know them, because they are spiritually discerned." (1 Corinthians 2:14-15). Our saving faith precedes the miracle of the receipt of spiritual gifts.

Our Heavenly Father is anxious to bless us with spiritual gifts. Without interfering with our agency, these gifts are sufficient to guide us to make behavioral lifestyle choices that are consistent with celestial principles. God is heavily invested in our success strategies. He wants us to pass

the individual tests of mortality, that we might move on to our celestial home, having satisfied the entrance requirements for admittance to His kingdom. With what greater gifts could our Heavenly Father bless us than with those that help us to reach our potential?

We cannot purchase spiritual gifts with the treasures of the earth. Perhaps this is why in their efforts to obtain the sacred records, Lehi's sons were stripped of all their gold, silver, and other precious things. The task was to be accomplished

in the Lord's way, by the power of His mighty arm that is great in the sight of the faithful, but that has a terrible effect upon the wicked. As Alma asked: "Can ye dispute the power of God?" (Mosiah 27:16).

The gift of wisdom is given to those who press forward with complete dedication, feasting upon the word of Christ, receiving physical and spiritual strength and nourishment, and enduring to the end

with continuing responsibility and accountability. These are they who will find the hidden treasures of knowledge that have been promised by God.

The mysteries of God are those truths that can only be known by revelation from the Holy Ghost. When we hunger and thirst for these promised blessings,

the doctrine of the priesthood, as words of wisdom, will distill upon our souls as the dews from heaven, and the Holy Ghost will be our constant companion.

The gift of knowledge is given to those who seek "line upon line, precept upon precept." (D&C 98:12). Personal revelation is our ultimate source for understanding scripture and knowing God's will. "These

currents are part of the flowing fountain of the church. If we do not drink, if we die of thirst while only inches from the fountain, the fault comes down to us. For the free, full, flowing, living water is there." (Truman Madsen).

The gift of administration is given to those who discern correctly the services and agencies through which the Lord operates His church. The priesthood bridges the gulf between heaven and

earth, attests to the nature of God, confirms that the Lord's church is founded on unchanging principles, and the exercise of its authority illustrates that the requirements for obtaining salvation are the same for all.

Church organizations that operate on borrowed light are sometimes quite popular with people who seek form without substance, and who enjoy the relative ease of putting forth minimal

effort in organizations that make few demands for personal sacrifice. The church of Christ is powered by the Spirit, and gives vitality to the performance requirements that are associated with God's blessings.

When we think of the gift of speaking in tongues, the missionaries who serve throughout the world come to mind. We also remember the Nephite children

whom Jesus blessed. These received an endowment of spiritual power, as the Savior loosed "their tongues, and they" spoke "unto their fathers great and marvelous things." (3 Nephi 26:14).

One of the terrible consequences of the fascination of the world with Babylon is spiritual insensitivity. Isaiah clearly foresaw the Last Days, when he wrote: "Stay yourselves, and wonder; cry ye

out, and cry: they are drunken, but not with wine; they stagger, but not with strong drink. For the Lord hath poured out upon you the spirit of deep sleep, and hath closed your eyes: the prophets, and your rulers, and seers hath he covered." (Isaiah 29:9-11).

The gift of the interpretation of tongues may include the ability to comprehend scripture. As the Lord told Joseph Smith: "These words are not of men...but of me; wherefore, you shall testify they are of

me and not of man. For it is my voice which speaketh them unto you; for they are given by my Spirit unto you, and by my power you can read them one to another; and save it were by my power you could not have them." (D&C 18:34-35).

The gift of prophesy is "the testimony of Jesus." (Revelation 19:10). It follows that those who have received the spiritual gift of testimony are prophets, since testimony

can only be received by revelation from the Holy Ghost, and since prophecy consists of what we speak when we are moved upon by the Spirit.

We believe the Bible to be the word of God as far as it is translated correctly; we also believe the Book of Mormon to be the word of God.

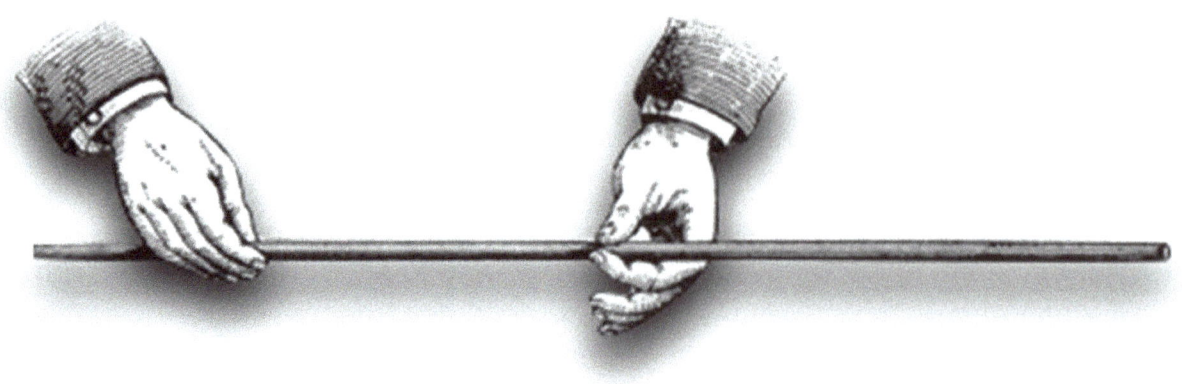

Long ago, in a psalm of lamentation, David cried: "Be merciful unto me, O God: for man would swallow me up... In God, I will praise his word; in God, I have put my trust; I will not fear what flesh can do unto me. Every day they

wrest my words." (Psalms 56:1-5). Those who wrest the scriptures pick them apart and distort the doctrine of Christ into meaningless fragments without any coherent connection. They fall into transgression in consequence of their shallow comprehension of principles.

Twisting of the meaning of doctrine is not a new phenomenon, and is the inevitable consequence of a shallow understanding of the principles of the gospel. Nephi foresaw that in the Last Days there would be many plain and precious things that had been taken

away from the book of the Lamb of God. As a result, there are many who seek the truth who stumble exceedingly, and are as the blind leading the blind. "And also many covenants of the Lord have they taken away." (1 Nephi 13:26).

Biblical prophecy teaches about apostasy by indirect reference, and begs for the restoration of truth, for "at the time the book proceeded out of the mouth of the

Jew, the things which were written were plain and pure, and most precious and easy to the understanding of all men." (1 Nephi 14:23).

The Lord said of the inhabitants of the earth: "They have strayed from mine ordinances, and have broken mine everlasting covenant. They seek not the Lord to establish his righteousness, but every man walketh in his own way,

and after the image of his own god, whose image is in the likeness of the world, and whose substance is that of an idol, which waxeth old and shall perish in Babylon, even Babylon the great, which shall fall." (D&C 1:15-16).

"For thus shall my church be called in the last days," declared the Lord, "even The Church of Jesus Christ of Latter-day Saints. Verily I say unto you all: Arise and shine forth, that thy light may be a standard for the nations." (D&C 115:4-

5). That light has the power to sweep away the gossamer threads of factious secular religion, obviating the need for different translations of the Bible. There will be one standard, and that will be the doctrine of Christ, as it is found in the holy scriptures.

"The rod of iron...was the word of God, which led to the fountain of living waters, or to the tree of life; which waters are a representation of the love of God; and (Nephi) also beheld that the tree of life was a representation of the love of God." (1 Nephi 11:25). Grounded by the rod of iron, the faithful need not

fear, although they may see many signs and wonders in heaven. The sinister equivalents of lightning may strike all around them, but they will be protected from harm by the "copper grid" of the scriptures that surrounds them and grounds them to the truth.

"Turn, all ye Gentiles, from your wicked ways; and repent of your evil doings, of your lyings and deceivings, and of your whoredoms, and of your secret abominations, and your idolatries, and of your murders, and your priestcrafts, and your envyings, and your strifes,

and from all your wickedness and abominations, and come unto me, and be baptized in my name, that ye may receive a remission of your sins, and be filled with the Holy Ghost, that ye may be numbered with my people who are of the house of Israel." (3 Nephi 30:2).

The Book of Mormon was preserved for our day so "every soul who belongs to

the whole human family of Adam (may) stand to be judged of (his or her) works, whether they be good or evil." (Mormon 3:20).

Moroni described conditions in the Last Days, when The Book of Mormon would come forth. It would be revealed in a day when people would be rational and self-reliant, and when they would say

that "miracles are done away." (Moroni 8:26). But the power of the book would be such that it would stir the soul and speak a language in harmony with the Spirit, "even as if one should speak from the dead." (Moroni 8:26).

Moroni clearly saw those in the Last Days who had "transfigured the holy word of God," who had changed the substance of the scriptures, and had so brought damnation upon their souls.

(Moroni 8:33). He foresaw that the way, the truth, and the life could be clearly found within the pages of The Book of Mormon.

The Book of Mormon was destined to come forth as the record of an ancient people whose voice would resonate with familiarity. "For those who shall be destroyed shall speak unto them out of the ground, and their speech shall

be low out of the dust, and their voice shall be as one that hath a familiar spirit; for the Lord God will give unto him power, that he may whisper concerning them, even as it were out of the ground; and their speech shall whisper out of the dust." (Isaiah 29:4).

Moroni specifically and pointedly wrote: "I speak unto you as if ye were present, and yet ye are not. But behold, Jesus Christ hath shown you unto me, and I know your doing." (Mormon 8:35).

Surely, what the Book of Mormon prophets wrote, and what Mormon abridged from their records, is of inestimable value to us. As Nephi said: "I have written what I have written, and I esteem it as of great worth." (2 Nephi 33:3). So should we, because The Book of Mormon was written and preserved for our day.

The Book of Mormon account of the effects in the New World of the crucifixion of the Savior provides a glimpse into the spiritual vacuum that will be experienced by those who have procrastinated their day of repentance. As Mormon reported: "There

was darkness upon the face of the land." (3 Nephi 8:19). So overpowering was the murky blackness, that "those who had not fallen could feel (its) vapor." The Spirit of Christ had been withdrawn; thus, "there could not be any light at all." The storm's survivors could see neither "the sun, nor the moon, nor the stars." (3 Nephi 8:20-22).

Alma wrote that the plates from which The Book of Mormon would be translated "must retain their brightness." Perhaps there is a dual meaning here. Metal plates that are soft enough to be easily inscribed upon tend to be less tarnish resistant. But also, the engravings

were to be preserved for those who would be struck by their simplicity. Perhaps Alma wanted to impress upon our minds that it is the substance, or the brightness of the message, that is clear, lucid, revealing, stunning, and eye-catching.

Many prophets have characterized gold as a symbol of the Celestial Kingdom's purity. Of his revelatory experience in the Kirtland Temple, Joseph Smith said: "We saw the Lord standing upon the breastwork of the pulpit, before us; and under his feet was a paved work of pure gold, in color like amber." (D&C 110:2).

In vision, Joseph F. Smith saw "the beautiful streets of that kingdom, which had the appearance of being paved with gold." (D&C 137:4). The Apostle John's experience was similar: "The street of the city was pure gold," he wrote, "as it were, transparent glass." (Revelation 21:21).

We believe all that God has revealed, all that He does now reveal, and we believe that He will yet reveal many great and important things pertaining to the Kingdom of God.

In the nineteenth century, the Prophet Joseph Smith was a witness to those seeking pure and undefiled religion, but even today he leads those who lack wisdom to the fountain of all truth. His presence dominates the history

of the Latter-day Saints. He has brought millions to the point where "they shall not teach every man his neighbour, and every man his brother, saying, Know the Lord. For all shall know me, from the least to the greatest." (Hebrews 8:11).

"I am the way, the truth, and the life: no man cometh unto the Father, but by me." (John 14:6). The Holy Ghost stirs us, as it were, from a deep sleep. Bathed in the stunning clarity of the Restoration, we stare in wide-eyed wonder at the

beautiful simplicity of the threads of gospel principles that are woven into the tapestry of the Plan of Salvation. As Jacob succinctly put it: "No man knoweth of (God's) ways, save it be revealed unto him." (Jacob 4:8).

From his birth to his martyr's death at the age of thirty-eight, Joseph Smith. "emerges the prophet, seer, organizer, lawgiver, promoter, architect, and teacher. His religious contributions

include fashioning the kingdom of God upon the earth, changing the lives of men and women, and preparing everyone who will listen, for Christ's advent." (Ivan Barrett).

"Wo unto him that shall deny the revelations of the Lord, and that shall say the Lord no longer worketh by

revelation, or by prophecy, or by gifts, or by tongues, or by healings, or by the power of the Holy Ghost!" (3 Nephi 29:6).

We have observed the disastrous consequences of disregard for the principles of the Plan. Particularly destructive are the habit patterns of those who are enslaved by drunkenness,

selfish indulgence, or intemperance. "O God, that men should put an enemy in their mouths to steal away their brains! That we should...transform ourselves into beasts!" (Shakespeare).

"No matter what ability and talent we may possess, all must come under this rule if we wish to know the Father and the Son. If knowledge of them is not obtained through revelation, it cannot be obtained at all." (John Taylor).

The light and knowledge we receive of God is given by personal revelation, when truth speaks directly to our souls. "For ye were sometimes darkness, but now are ye light in the Lord. Walk as children of light." (Ephesians 5:8).

Satan's false ideology is a recipe for disaster. It is the worst form of virulent infectious disease. When we venture into his realm, we enter the "Hot Zone." There is no greater crime than exposing God's children to the contagion of temptation, or of recruiting them by example into the

legions of the adversary. We cannot lower the bar by either compromise or complacency, in order to accommodate his corrupted counsel. The encouraging words of the Lord stir us: "I am the bread of life: He that cometh to me shall never hunger; and he that believeth on me shall never thirst." (John 6:35).

Many people in the world deny themselves the blessings of heaven simply because they do not know how to ask for them. The Savior explained that our Heavenly Father is anxious to grant the righteous requests of His children. Comparing His

matchless benevolence to our well-intentioned but weak efforts, the Son of God declared: "How much more shall your Father who is in heaven give good things to them that ask him?" (3 Nephi 14:11).

Members of the Lord's church are taught to take heed and to pray always. As Shakespeare famously wrote: "What's past is prologue." That is to say, our experiences are merely a foreshadowing of that which is to come. Over millennia,

things have not changed much. The main reason for the scriptures, after all, is to persuade us to believe in Christ. Thus, the prophets all seem to sound alike, for they draw upon the same eternal truths to make their points. Theirs is not just vain repetition; it is theatrical encore.

God will continue to reveal many great and important things pertaining to the kingdom. He sends us tenderly crafted love letters with words of encouragement, hoping that they will be opened and read

with care, and then safeguarded in the treasury of our hearts and minds. These lines of communication become avenues of a freely flowing correspondence between heaven and earth.

True professors of religion are faithful, persevering, and focused on the tasks at hand. They begin with the end in mind, settle for more, and not for less; are not easily distracted or persuaded, and are purposeful, determined, and disciplined.

Their foundation is on bedrock. They have depth and breadth, and they have reserves in spiritual bank accounts to which they have made regular deposits, and from which they may take strategic withdrawals in times of need.

Picking apart the scriptures can distort dogma into meaningless fragments without any coherent connection, and it can also redefine doctrine into nonsensical and bizarre definitions. In the spring of 1820, the Lord characterized such individuals as those who "draw near to me with their lips, but (whose) hearts are far from me. They

teach for doctrines the commandments of men, having a form of godliness, but they deny the power thereof." (J.S.H. 2:19). They rely on their own puny efforts instead of upon the boundless grace of God for their salvation, reducing the Plan of Salvation to a crude caricature devoid of meaning or substance.

The true doctrine of Christ has been clearly revealed. Anything less is of evil, because it keeps the children of men from reaching their potential by denying them the opportunity to be obedient to the laws of the Great Plan of Salvation.

The keystone of His doctrine is His grace that is extended to all who merit salvation through faith on His name. That which is expected of His disciples focuses solely on strict adherence to the principles, and participation in the ordinances, of His gospel.

After we have been taught correct principles, we are left to govern our behavior according to the light and knowledge we have received. We must always take care to watch our thoughts, our words, and our deeds. The Lord will always give us overall

objectives and guidelines to follow, but He expects us to work out most of the details ourselves. These are developed through study and prayer, and are given vitality by the promptings of the Spirit.

We believe in the literal gathering of Israel and in the restoration of the Ten Tribes; that Zion (the new Jerusalem) will be built upon the American continent; that Christ will reign personally upon the earth; and, that the earth will be renewed and receive its paradisiacal glory.

In the eyes of the Lord, the earth has been corrupted, is ruined, and is no longer fit for sacred use. It has been made dirty and is polluted, "under the

inhabitants thereof; because they have transgressed the laws, changed the ordinance, (and have) broken the everlasting covenant" (Isaiah 24:5).

Most people think of the Jews when referring to the Gathering. However, they represent but one of the Twelve Tribes. "For lo...I will sift the house of Israel among all nations." (Amos 9:9). Isaiah said the Lord would set His hand a second time to gather His people. As he saw it, the House of Israel would

return from the seven known countries of his day, "from Assyria, and from Egypt, and from Pathros (upper Egypt), and from Cush (Ethiopia), and from Elam (east of Babylonia), and from Hamath (Northern Syria), and from the isles of the sea" (the rest of the world). (2 Nephi 21:11, see Isaiah 11:11).

At the millennial day, all the world shall lift up its voice as one, and sing, declaring that "the earth hath travailed and brought forth her strength," as a mother who has borne a new child, "and the heavens have smiled upon her," for she is pure and delightsome. "And she is

clothed with the glory of her God," that is to say, she is adorned in the strength of His priesthood. "For he stands in the midst of his people (with) glory, and honor, and power, and might. For he is full of mercy, justice, grace and truth, and peace." (D&C 84:101-102).

Although few of us may consciously recognize it, we enjoy a mystical bond with the land itself. In a bold statement reminiscent of the predominant message of The Book of Mormon, President Lyndon B. Johnson said of his forbearers: "They came to America to make a

covenant with this land. Conceived in justice, written in liberty, bound in union, it was meant one day to inspire the hopes of all mankind, and it binds us still. If we keep its terms, we shall flourish."

There are many who are lost from the knowledge of those who are at Jerusalem. Nevertheless, "the Lord God will proceed to make bare his arm in the eyes of all the nations, in bringing about his covenants and his gospel unto those who are of the house of Israel. Wherefore, he will bring them again out of captivity,

and they shall be gathered together to the lands of their inheritance; and they shall be brought out of obscurity and out of darkness; and they shall know that the Lord is their Savior and their Redeemer, the Mighty One of Israel" (1 Nephi 22:11-12).

The Lord revealed to Joseph Smith: "They who are in the north countries shall come in remembrance before the Lord; and their prophets shall hear his voice,

and shall no longer stay themselves; and they shall smite the rocks, and the ice shall flow down at their presence. And an highway shall be cast up in the midst of the great deep." (D&C 133:26-27).

Esdras described the escape from Assyria of the lost Tribes of Israel: "Those are the ten tribes, which were carried away prisoners out of their own land in the time of Hosea...whom Salmanasar the king of Assyria led away captive, and he carried them over the waters, and so came they into another land. But

they took this counsel among themselves, that they would leave the multitude of the heathen, and go forth unto a further country where never mankind dwelt, that they might there keep their statutes, which they never kept in their own land." (Apocrypha, 2 Esdras 13:40-47).

Even though conditions in the world will degenerate and peace will be taken from the wicked, those in Zion will enjoy the safety and security that only

righteousness can guarantee, and there will be such an outpouring of the Spirit that "the earth shall be full of the knowledge of the Lord, as the waters cover the sea." (Isaiah 11:9).

We do not need to wait for the Millennium for the Holy Ghost to be poured out in rich abundance, and for priesthood-directed teaching and gospel instruction to be

widely available. For these things "shall be revealed" today, even "in the days of the dispensation of the fulness of times." (D&C 121:31).

On the millennial earth, the stylus of our compass will be set on the purification process, and a circle will be scribed within which will be the sacrament, the endowment, and the other ordinances driven by the engine of the priesthood.

Ordinances and their related covenants have the power to generate godliness, and the active participation of the Saints in these rites will typify the cleansing and refining process described in the scriptures that allows them to bask in the presence of the Lord.

On the millennial earth, time as we now know it will no longer be our natural dimension. It will have served its purpose as the steady and methodical taskmaster that aforetime had ceaselessly motivated us to move forward toward our eternal destiny. Growing old in the telestial world may simply have been a device

created by God that afforded us an opportunity to gauge the approach of our reunion with Him in the terrestrial world. We will realize that its subtle passage had the power to make of us saints or sinners. and that it had been up to us all along, during our probationary state, to decide which path we would follow.

During the Millennium, the Saints may look forward to the time of their lives. They will rejoice that they heeded the warning that "in an hour when ye think not the summer shall be past, and the harvest ended." (D&C 45:2). Our vision of the Millennium was created by Orientals who were not architects, but artists. These prophets painted scenes

whose totality was true, but whose details may have been inaccurate. In contrast, as Occidentals, we are accustomed to drawing diagrams that are correct in every respect, but at the expense of vibrancy in their texture. In short, we will likely be very pleasantly surprised by what we find on the millennial earth.

No one can deny the great power in the imagery of Hebrew poetry, particularly as it relates to the millennial earth. It steals music from the morning stars, and speaks of a bridegroom who needs no lamp oil. Its snows are undefiled, and it

drives the clouds in the sky. It rules the raging sea, and rides on the wings of the wind. It makes gold seem richer, myrrh more fragrant, and frankincense sweeter. The flocks of its shepherds are safely bedded down in green pastures and its barrels of meal will never waste.

We think of the universality of God's love for all of His children, particularly as it relates to the millennial earth. "He inviteth them all to come unto him and

partake of his goodness; and he denieth none that come unto him, black and white, bond and free, male and female; and he remembereth the heathen; and all are alike unto God, both Jew and Gentile." (2 Nephi 26:33).

On the paradisiacal earth, time will take on a new meaning. No longer will we spend it unwisely, or get "held up" at the office. When we ask someone to "give us a minute," we will realize that it is within our power to manipulate the arrow of time to the benefit of Zion. With new-fund respect and reverence,

and with our enjoyment of its multiple layers of meaning, we will promote the cause of millennial society by the careful thought with which we spend our time, the diligence with which we make time, the care with which we find time, and the discipline with which we take time.

We claim the privilege of worshiping Almighty God according to the dictates of our own conscience, and allow all men the same privilege, let them worship how, where, or what they may.

"The bosom of America is open to receive the oppressed and persecuted of all nations and religions, whom we shall welcome to a participation of all our rights and privileges.

They may be Mohometans, Jews, or Christians of any sect, or they may be atheists." (George Washington).

Many people are only aware of Act Two of the Three Act Play (the Plan of Salvation: Where did we come from? Why are we here? Where are we going?). Somehow, their religious educational system has been broken. They behave as though they skipped kindergarten and don't recognize the need for college level courses. They are as the honorable

men and women among the sects, parties and denominations, "who are blinded by the subtle craftiness of men (who) lie in wait to deceive." Many who would be drawn to the light "are only kept from the truth because they know not where to find it." (D&C 76:75 & 123:12).

Fading light is the consequence of the corrosive nature of sin, which is the uglier part of the opposition in all things that is necessary for the Plan's successful execution. Without baptism, which is its lynchpin, all is lost.

Fortunately, the Lord reveals truth to those who are spiritually prepared to understand it, and from the beginning has provided an illuminated pathway, that all might walk without stumbling.

Free will, or agency, which is the power to choose, is the crowning principle of creation. "Therefore, cheer up your hearts, and remember that ye are free to act for yourselves - to choose the

way of everlasting death, or the way of eternal life." (2 Nephi 10:23). We may, choose, but we cannot escape the consequences that follow.

Abraham Lincoln once said he did not worry whether God was on his side, or not. "For I know that the Lord is always on the side of the right. It is my constant anxiety and prayer," he

continued, "that both I and this nation should be on the Lord's side.'" "Choose you this day whom ye will serve," declared Joshua, "but as for me and my house, we will serve the Lord." (Joshua 24:15).

"The liberality and virtue of America in establishing perfect equality and freedom among all religious societies, will no doubt produce to us a great reward, for when news of it reaches

oppressed dissenters from the churches of Europe, and they find it encourages both Protestants and Catholics, they will at once cry out, America is the Land of Promise." (Tench Coxe, 1778, Continental Congress delegate from Pennsylvania).

"And that law of the land which is constitutional, supporting that principle of freedom in maintaining rights and privileges, belongs to all mankind, and is justifiable before me. Therefore, I, the Lord, justify you, and your brethren

of my church, in befriending that law which is the constitutional law of the land; and as pertaining to law of man, whatsoever is more or less than this, cometh of evil." (D&C 98:5-7).

Those who are stiff-necked lack the faith that would bless them with pliancy, plasticity, perception, and perspective, and that would allow them to be influenced by the Holy Ghost, "which maketh manifest unto the children of men." (Jarom 1:4). Inflexibility prevents

us from looking up to Heavenly Father for guidance, over to priesthood leaders for counsel, around to seek out those in need, or down in humility. When we are born again, our necks will bear up our heads with a refreshing spiritual elasticity.

Teaching others who may not believe as we do is multi-faceted and is conducted on many levels and in many different settings. One style may be appropriate to one circumstance, while another approach may be tailor-made to fit another situation. We are all at

different stages in the journey of our spiritual awakening, and what is meaningful for one may not be for another. The common denominator for every variable is that our teachings is endowed with spiritual sensitivity.

Our role-models are the Sons of Mosiah, who "had waxed strong in the knowledge of the truth; for they were men of a sound understanding and they had searched the scriptures diligently, that they might know the word of God.

But this is not all; they had given themselves to much prayer, and fasting; therefore they had the spirit of prophecy, and the spirit of revelation, and when they taught, they taught with power and authority of God." (Mosiah 17:2-3).

We tread on stable ground when the scriptures are the basis or foundation of gospel scholarship; indeed, as Mormon observed of Alma's teaching efforts:

"The preaching of the word had a great tendency to lead the people to do that which was just; yea, it had more powerful effect upon the minds of the people than the sword, or anything else." (Alma 31:5).

Pondering the scriptures fosters both intellectual and spiritual unity. When it is strengthened by a study of the expanding library of Latter-day Saint publications, a fortress of faith is created. The glory of God is

intelligence, by whatever avenue that light and truth may come to us. Henry Thoreau echoed the prophets when he said: "Books are the treasured wealth of the world and the fit inheritance of generations and nations."

With humility, memorable teachers are able to awaken in us the sense that our "birth is but a sleep and a forgetting," and that "the soul that rises with us, our life's star, hath had elsewhere its setting, and cometh from

afar." They have the capacity to touch tender chords that resonate with the truth that "not in utter nakedness, but trailing clouds of glory do we come, from God, Who is our Home." (William Wordsworth).

The strength of the church lies in the interactive communication with God of its individual members. Theirs is an overflowing of energy that is a

reflection of their joyous approach to life. They are quickened by the Spirit, and enthusiastically recognize the source of the life-sustaining water that nourishes them.

Many honorable people are only kept from the truth because they do not know where to find it. They are deceived by Satan, who uses telestial toys that are the corruptible treasures of the earth, as weak counterfeits of God. These

stand in opposition to celestial sureties and the imperishable riches of eternity. As Jeremiah asked: "Shall a man make gods unto himself, and they are no gods?" (Jeremiah 16:20).

We believe in being subject to kings, presidents, rulers, and magistrates, in obeying, honoring, and sustaining the law.

A statement made by Thomas Paine in "Common Sense," over 200 years ago strikes a familiar chord with Latter-day Saints today. He wrote: "We have it in our power to begin the world over again. A situation similar to the present has not

happened since the days of Noah." The Saints believe in "a serene Providence which rules the fate of nations. It makes its own instruments, creates the man for the time...inspires his genius, and arms him for his task." (Ralph Waldo Emerson).

The Latter-day Saint statement of belief recognizing the rule of law underscores the warning of Teddy Roosevelt that "discrimination against the holder of one faith leads to retaliatory discrimination

against those of other faiths. The result is an abandonment of our freedom of conscience and a reversion to religious dissention which in so many lands has proven fatal to true liberty, to true religion, and to advances in civilization."

Sandra Day O'Conner wrote: "The goal of the Religion Clauses in the Constitution is clear. It is to carry out the Founders' plan of preserving religious liberty in a pluralistic society. The Clauses preserve religion as a matter for individual conscience, not for the prosecutor or the bureaucrat. At a time when we see

in other parts of the world the violent consequences of the assumption of religious authority by government, Americans may count themselves fortunate. Our regard for constitutional boundaries has protected us from similar travails, while allowing private religious exercise to flourish."

"Mormons are like artichokes. At first encounter, you either like them or you don't. But those who have unfavorable first impressions often find that once the outer layers are peeled away, both Mormons and artichokes are most enjoyable. In fact, most people who

get to know Mormons become their friends A little objective research on Mormon beliefs reveals that, except for a few doctrinal differences, those who call themselves Latter-day Saints are just like the rest of us...very human beings." ("The Boston Globe," 1967)

As the end of the world approaches, the church is co-operating with the gentile nations of the earth to facilitate the gathering of Israel. "Thus saith the Lord God: Behold, I will lift up mine hand to the Gentiles, and set up my standard to the people; and they shall bring thy sons

in their arms, and thy daughters shall be carried upon their shoulders." (Isaiah 49:22). The ensign to which the people will look is the gospel standard, which is the ultimate rule of law in a theocratic society.

Until a Zion society is created and the celestial character trait of consecration is irrevocably woven into the fibers of our being, we must tolerate leaders who are "supported in their laziness, and in their idolatry, and in their whoredoms, by the taxes which (are) put upon the

people." Unfortunately, when the people labor to support such iniquity, they may also become infected by idolatry as they are "deceived by the vain and flattering words of (their) kings and priests." (Mosiah 11:6-7).

The gospel focuses our thoughts, our words, and our deeds on laws that deal with accountability, brotherhood, equality, agency, selflessness, charity, stewardship, and consecration. It is akin to celestial

aroma-therapy for those who have become mired in telestial trappings. "How carefully most of us creep into nameless graves," observed Phillips Brooks, "while now and again one or two forget themselves into immortality."

Before the Second Coming of the Lord, profane government will be destroyed, because its concept of welfare is defined only by a detached, disinterested, and

ineffectual temporal paternalism, with an economic baseline that too often ignores the worth of souls. This is in contrast to the active, meaningful brotherhood and spiritual unity that defines the character of the inhabitants of Zion.

The Saints trust in the Lord because they have experienced the illumination that comes from easy access to the Spirit. With it comes confirmation, as they begin to feel the effects of their devotions in their daily lives. Fully

taking advantage of the exhilarating learning laboratory of mortality, they find in the gospel of Jesus Christ the courage to live with a confidence born of righteousness that is independent of circumstances.

Covenant Israel has learned a thing or two about sustaining the law. She knows that when she does, she "shall flourish like the palm tree: she shall grow like a cedar in Lebanon. Those that be planted in the house of the Lord shall flourish in the courts of our God." (Psalms 92:12-

13). Israel will thrive in the midst of surroundings that appear to be desert wastes. However, beneath the literal and figurative surface layers of rock and sand, she has discovered the nourishment of oases that are constantly replenished by the underlying currents of living water that were described by the Savior to the woman at the well.

When members of the Lord's church zealously live in harmony with gospel principles and the true doctrine of the kingdom, the character of the societies in which they are embedded begins to change. One early observer

of The Church of Jesus Christ of Latter-day Saints predicted: "If it could be true to its foundations and remain unchanged for four generations, it might well become the most powerful social influence in the world." (Leo Tolstoy).

Oh, how foolish most of us are when we get a whiff of fame, a taste of fortune, or fancy ourselves as celebrities, while all the time, the character of Heavenly Father reposes above the fray, and

stands unblemished. It is He alone Who deserves a theatrical encore, and Who, at the end of Act Two of the Three Act Play, will receive kneeling ovations from the supporting cast that is made up of His children.

God is alive and well and is not hiding under an assumed name in Argentina, as some have supposed. He continues to enjoy tremendous popularity. His book is still on the best-seller list. In fact, it

has enjoyed such success that He has authored several additional volumes, and it is rumored that He is in the final stages of negotiation for new book deals.

We wish that all governments mirrored the law of heaven, whose power stems from love. Far too often, however, temporal authority feeds on the elusive and transient counterfeit from hell that is driven by greed, avarice, lust, and

the unrighteous desire for dominion. It is not very difficult to identify the fingerprints of Satan, smeared all over the programs, policies, pronouncements, proclamations, politics, plans, and parties that promote paltry, petty, provincial, and personal agendas.

In contrast to our considerable influence over conduct of temporal government, we are completely helpless to alter God's affairs. It was when Moses realized his utter dependence upon God that he exclaimed: "Now, for this cause I know that man is nothing, which thing I never had supposed." (Moses 1:10). His

debt to God was total and complete. Benjamin asked: "Can ye say aught of yourselves? Nay. Ye cannot say that ye are even as much as the dust of the earth; yet ye were created of the dust of the earth; but behold, it belongeth to him who created you." (Mosiah 2:25).

We believe in being honest, true, chaste, benevolent, virtuous, and in doing good to all men; indeed, we may say that we follow the admonition of Paul — We believe all things, we hope all things, and we have endured many things, and hope to be able to endure all things.

If there is anything virtuous, lovely, or of good report or praiseworthy, we seek after these things.

The 13th Article of Faith encourages us to adopt character traits toward which our efforts have carried us. Their acquisition cannot be purchased at any price. Instead they have a performance cost. Those who

desire to improve their nature must invest everything they are, including their trust, confidence, expectations, convictions, and assurance, as well as their anticipation that the Lord will surely deliver on His promises.

"At this moment, I have in my heart a prayer. As I have assumed my duties, I humbly pray to Almighty God, in the words of King Solomon: 'Give therefore Thy servant an understanding heart to judge Thy people, that I may discern

between good and bad.' I ask only to be a good and faithful servant of my Lord and of my people." (Harry S. Truman, in his first address to Congress following the death of President Franklin D. Roosevelt.)

Living water is so crucial to our well-being that the Lord has provided a channel that can penetrate hundreds of feet of solid limestone, as it were, so that it may freely flow into our lives. With great effort, this conduit through our rough exterior and stony nature is

chiseled with the tools of faith, study, obedience, prayer, good works, and healthy lifestyle choices. Our access to living water is created when we are honest, pure, chaste, benevolent, and kind; and when we are virtuous and do good to others.

Gospel links forge an unbreakable relationship with God. The covenants we make with Him are the keystones of our success because they define the bounds and conditions that allow us to emulate Him. They reveal His nature and reflect His attributes. Our covenants

address morality, chastity, obedience, charity, discipline, sacrifice, stewardship, and consecration. The ordinances of the gospel and our covenants are the tools that make "eternal progression" possible.

We believe in every principle that uplifts, motivates, encourages, and inspires us to be better. The future is bright because the Light of the World and the Hope of Israel is always there to lead us by His shining example. He comforts us in the

trials of life, as we endure to the end in righteousness. If we can discover anything that is virtuous, lovely, or of good report or praiseworthy, we seek after these things, because, at the end of the day, light cleaves unto light and intelligence to intelligence.

We commit the Golden Rule not only to memory, but also to life itself. We are justifiably proud of our honesty with our fellow men, as well as with ourselves. We are true to proven principles of behavior, faithful to our covenants, and we do good and spread

cheer no matter the circumstances in which we may find ourselves. We take our cues from the inside, rather than from external influences. Our common identity allows us to stand with the church, independent of all creatures.

The scriptures teach us that we should seek living water diligently; that we should teach each other words of wisdom out of the best books, and seek learning, even by study and also by faith. Obedience to the principles of the gospel helps us to

prepare every needful thing, and to shine like beacons of hope in the midst of spiritual Babylon. We have the tools to establish a house of prayer, a house of fasting, a house of faith, a house of learning, a house of order, and even a house of God. (See D&C 88:118-119).

Any connection to standards that the world might have had has toppled over onto the shifting sands of situational ethics. The world's moral compass is spinning wildly because it is no longer centered on unchanging principles of

righteous living. Instead, it has embraced the rationalization that the end justifies the means. It has turned from true and correct principles at the risk of the loss of personal freedom now and eternal life later. It has traded its birthright for a mess of porridge.

When we establish a house of glory, a house of order, and a house of God, our incomings will be in the name of the Lord, as well as our outgoings. Our salutations will be made with uplifted hands, as we praise the Most High. As

we refresh ourselves with His living water, we will cease from all our light speeches, from amusement at the expense of others, from lustful desire, from pride and light mindedness, and from all wickedness.

It is self-evident that covenants are received only by revelation. Since they are binding contracts with God, they must come through profound two-way communication with Him. It follows that we cannot make holy covenants without direct revelation from heaven. That being said, the only ones who may do

so are those who believe that the heavens are open, and that revelation continues to guide those who seek fellowship in the Lord's church and kingdom. Covenants prosper His loyal and faithful disciples who acknowledge not only His legitimate rule but also His interactive involvement with His children.

"Seek ye first the kingdom of God, and His righteousness, and all these things shall be added unto you." (Matthew 6:33). Seeking God's gifts is more than wishful thinking. It is not a misguided trust in promises that cannot be fulfilled. God does not write checks that His disciples cannot cash. Our hope is the reasonable

expectation of promised blessings that flow from obedience; the inevitable reward of well-founded faith. His gifts represent the interest that has been earned on an investment made in undeviating trust in God and in the principles of the gospel of Jesus Christ.

We are the architects of our own fate, even as we draw upon powers greater than ourselves to review and stamp the blueprints of life. How wonderful is it to be blessed with strong testimonies, so that when we fall, as we inevitably will, heaven will attend us, and we will know

to Whom it is that we may turn, that we may be enveloped in His protective arms and set back upon our feet. "I will go before your face," promised the Lord, and "will be on your right hand, and on your left, and my Spirit shall be in your hearts, and mine angels round about you, to bear you up." (D&C 84:88).

We set our course, and move along it. The restored gospel of Jesus Christ illuminates the pathway. The church administers the ordinances and builds upon the rock of continuing revelation that is buttressed by the marvelous power of testimony. Our collective

witness is greater than the sum of its parts. And so, asked Joseph Smith: "Shall we not go on in so great a cause? Go forward, and not backward. Courage, brethren; and on, on to the victory! Let your hearts rejoice, and be exceedingly glad." (D&C 128:22).

The Lord encourages us to be faithful, to be bright with hope, to abound in charity, and to embrace the noble characteristics of "virtue, knowledge, temperance,

patience, brotherly kindness, godliness, humility, (and) diligence." (D&C 4:6). We do this, "that we might be partakers of the divine nature." (2 Peter 1:4). In all that we do, we "look to God, and (when we do, we) live." (Alma 37:47).

Truly, did Paul declare: "God hath not given us the spirit of fear, but of power, and of love, and of a sound mind." (2 Timothy 1:7). Testimony is blessed by a grateful heart and by a love that only an uncluttered mind may express. It is

a manifestation of our understanding from the source of all knowledge, and of our desire to act upon what is right instead of what is expedient. As Peter said: "We ought to obey God rather than men. (Acts 5:29). Testimony blesses us to become as little children, pure and without guile.

About the Author

Phil Hudson and Jan, his wife of 49 years, have 7 children and over 20 grandchildren. They enjoy spending time with their family at their cabin nestled along the Selkirk Crest, on the

shore of Priest Lake, the crown jewel of North Idaho. Phil is at the stage of his life where he tries to act upon the wise counsel of his children. This book is the result of their suggestion to provide his grandchildren with an opportunity to better understand his perspective on the Articles of Faith of the church. At the time of its publication, he and Jan were preparing to leave on a church mission to the Kingdom of Tonga.

If time permits, Phil's future writing projects will include a book of essays chronicling his life experiences, as well as a volume of commentary relating to his favorite scriptures.

www.ingramcontent.com/pod-product-compliance
Lightning Source LLC
Chambersburg PA
CBHW042359280426
43661CB00096B/1168